🕮 READERS

Level 2

Level 3

A Note to Parents

DK READERS is a compelling program for beginning readers, designed in conjunction with leading literacy experts, including Dr. Linda Gambrell, Professor of Education at Clemson University. Dr. Gambrell has served as President of the National Reading Conference, the College Reading Association, and the International Reading Association.

Beautiful illustrations and superb full-color photographs combine with engaging, easy-to-read stories and informational texts to offer a fresh approach to each subject in the series. Each DK READER is guaranteed to capture a child's interest while developing his or her reading skills, general knowledge, and love of reading.

The five levels of DK READERS are aimed at different reading abilities, enabling you to choose the books that are exactly right for your child:

Pre-level 1: Learning to read
Level 1: Beginning to read
Level 2: Beginning to read alone
Level 3: Reading alone
Level 4: Proficient readers

The "normal" age at which a child begins to read can be anywhere from three to eight years old. Adult participation through the lower levels is very helpful for providing encouragement, discussing storylines, and sounding out unfamiliar words.

No matter which level you select, you can be sure that you are helping your child learn to read, then read to learn!

LONDON, NEW YORK,
MELBOURNE, MUNICH, AND DELHI

For DK/BradyGames
Global Strategy Guide Publisher
Mike Degler
Digital and Trade Category Publisher
Brian Saliba
Editor-In-Chief
H. Leigh Davis

Operations Manager
Stacey Beheler
Title Manager
Tim Fitzpatrick
Book Designer
Tim Amrhein

For DK Publishing
Publishing Director
Beth Sutinis
Licensing Editor
Nancy Ellwood

Reading Consultant
Linda B. Gambrell, Ph.D.

DK/BradyGAMES
800 East 96th St., 3rd floor
Indianapolis, IN 46240

11 12 13 10 9 8 7 6 5 4 3 2 1

A catalog record for this book is available from the Library of Congress.

ISBN: 978-0-7566-7603-2 (Paperback)

ISBN: 978-0-7566-8702-1 (Hardback)

Printed and bound by Lake Book

Discover more at

www.dk.com

DK READERS

BEGINNING
2
TO READ ALONE

Meet Ash's Pikachu!

Written by Michael Teitelbaum

DK Publishing

Ash Ketchum is a 10-year-old boy from Pallet Town. Ash loves Pokémon. His goal is to become a Pokémon Master. Ash was very

Say hello to Pikachu!

lucky. For his first Pokémon, Ash got a Pikachu!

Through his friendship with Pikachu, Ash learned that caring for your Pokémon is more important than how many you catch. Helping your Pokémon grow is much more important than how many battles it wins.

However, this doesn't mean Ash and Pikachu had an easy start when they first met!

Ash was very excited about getting his first Pokémon from Professor Oak. However, on the morning he was supposed to choose his first Pokémon, Ash slept too late!

Ash Ketchum and Pikachu make a great pair!

Ash ran as fast as he could to Professor Oak's lab. By the time he arrived, there was only one Pokémon left: Pikachu. So Ash chose the small, yellow, Electric-type Pokémon.

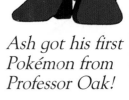

Ash got his first Pokémon from Professor Oak!

Just think; if Ash had not overslept, he might have chosen another Pokémon. One of the great friendships in Pokémon history might have never happened!

Ash and Pikachu meet for the first time!

Once Ash chose Pikachu, he was ready to try to capture his first wild Pokémon. However, to catch a wild Pokémon, a Pokémon Trainer needs to battle it first. Ash needed Pikachu's help.

The trouble was, Pikachu didn't fully trust Ash. In fact, at first, Pikachu kept zapping Ash with electric shocks. Pikachu also refused to go into Ash's Poké Ball.

However, as their journey continued, a flock of Spearow attacked. They wanted to harm Pikachu. Ash showed his strength as he stopped the Spearow and saved Pikachu.

Spearow

Ash rushed Pikachu to a Pokémon Center, where Pikachu recovered from the attack. At that moment, Pikachu finally realized how much Ash cared for it.

Nurse Joy helped Pikachu recover.

n time, Ash cared so much that he
ven offered his Pikachu a chance to
ive free in a forest filled with other
'ikachu. However, Ash's Pikachu
hose to stay with him. The two
rew closer and closer from that
oint onward!

Pikachu's Moves
Ash's Pikachu has learned some powerful moves.
A few of this Electric-type Pokémon's best-known
moves are Quick Attack, Thunderbolt, Volt Tackle,
and Iron Tail.

Pikachu uses Volt Tackle against Raichu!

It was not easy for Ash to train Pikachu, especially because Ash had never trained a Pokémon before. As he got to know Pikachu better, Ash learned a key rule of being a good Pokémon Trainer: if a Pokémon Trainer trusts his or her Pokémon, the Pokémon will come to trust the Trainer.

The more challenges Ash and Pikachu faced together, the deeper their trust grew.

In battle, Pikachu always fights as hard as it can!

Their friendship got stronger and soon they were a team. Eventually they became best friends, and they wouldn't have it any other way.

Pikachu fights fiercely, especially for those it cares about, like Ash! Pikachu usually isn't shy. However, when it's around Dawn's Buneary,

Dawn's Buneary has a crush on Pikachu!

brave Pikachu sometimes becomes downright shy. That's because Buneary has a huge crush on Pikachu!

Pikachu may be small. It can occasionally be shy, but Pikachu is a fierce competitor when it comes to Pokémon battles. Time and again it has conquered overwhelming odds in battle. Because Ash's Pikachu always gives one hundred percent, it has defeated many Pokémon that seemed to be much more powerful. Pikachu's devotion to Ash helps it to fight and win for its Pokémon Trainer.

Pikachu defeated Flint's Infernape and Volkner's Luxray!

Zapped!

When Pikachu gets low on energy, sometimes a huge electrical jolt, like getting hit by a lightning bolt, is just what it needs to get back into battle-ready condition. However, if too much electricity builds up in its body and it can't release that extra energy, Pikachu can get feverish and sick. This problem sometimes happens to Electric-type Pokémon.

Pikachu once charged up with lightning to battle Elekid!

13

In a tough battle against a Milotic, Ash came up with a creative plan to help his Pikachu win a battle against an opponent that appeared to be more powerful.

Milotic spun into a Twister move, which created a whirlpool around it.

Milotic

Pikachu springs into action!

Then, in a decision that surprised everyone, Ash called for Pikachu to run straight into the Twister. Once inside the Twister, Pikachu used Volt Tackle at maximum power. This bold, inventive move left Milotic unable to battle. Pikachu was the winner!

Another time, in the Sinnoh region, Pikachu helped Ash after he lost his first Gym battle with Gym Leader Roark. After the loss, Ash and Pikachu saw Dawn training her Pokémon to use special spinning moves for their next Contest.

Go, Pikachu, go!

That gave Ash an idea. In his next battle with Roark, Roark's Onix unleashed Double-Edge against Pikachu.

Ash told Pikachu to use a spin to dodge the attack. Pikachu's move built up a lot of wind pressure, forming a cushion of spinning air. The air cushion softened the blow from Onix. Once again, Ash's and Pikachu's cleverness helped Pikachu in battle!

Pikachu took down Roark's Onix!

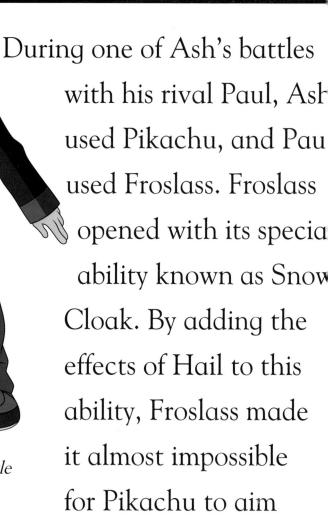

During one of Ash's battles with his rival Paul, Ash used Pikachu, and Paul used Froslass. Froslass opened with its special ability known as Snow Cloak. By adding the effects of Hail to this ability, Froslass made it almost impossible for Pikachu to aim

Paul sent his Froslass to battle Ash's Pikachu!

any of its attacks. That's because the hail could hide Froslass from view, allowing it to suddenly appear and disappear almost like a ghost!

Pikachu countered with Thunderbolt, but missed because it couldn't see Froslass in all the hail. Froslass was so well hidden that Pikachu couldn't land an attack. Then, Froslass trapped Pikachu with Ice Beam. Once more, Pikachu's cleverness came to the rescue. Pikachu used Volt Tackle, smashed its way out of the ice, and won the match!

Froslass tried hard, but Pikachu found a way to win!

Ash takes great care of his Pikachu, but sometimes Pikachu takes care of others. One time, on a steamboat to Sinnoh's Hearthome City, Pikachu showed its brave and caring side.

The steamboat drifted out onto the river. Lots of Pokémon were onboard, but no people were on the boat.

Pikachu helped watch over Brock's Happiny and Dawn's Pachirisu!

While the Pokémon played on the boat, Pikachu worked hard to keep them from falling into the river.

Pikachu also stopped the Pokémon from breaking all kinds of things they knocked over. When the boat was about to crash, Pikachu helped get the littlest Pokémon off the boat to safety. Pikachu then smashed the rock that was in the boat's path.

Pikachu Pretends
Because of its loyalty to Ash, Pikachu will do whatever is necessary to help. On one occasion, this included pretending to be an old lady's Pikachu!

Despite its skill and cleverness, Ash's Pikachu does not win every battle. However, even in the face of defeat, Pikachu never gives up and is always up for a

Drifblim defeated Pikachu, but Pikachu never gives up

rematch. One time, Pikachu lost to Gym Leader Fantina's Drifblim. Did that stop Pikachu from being ready to battle Drifblim again? Not at all!

Another time, Ash was battling Paul. Ash chose Pikachu, and Paul chose Magmortar. Again Pikachu lost, but it was immediately ready for a rematch. The same thing happened when Pikachu battled Elite Four Flint's Infernape and when it battled Gym Leader Volkner's Luxray. Whatever the competition, whatever the battle—win or lose, Pikachu is always ready to go another round!

Pikachu went toe to toe with Paul's Magmortar!

Some Pikachu can't wait to evolve into Raichu, but not Ash's Pikachu. It has had chances to evolve into Raichu. These chances came after Raichu defeated it in battle. Nevertheless, Ash's Pikachu has always decided not to evolve because it's happy and likes winning battles just the way it is.

Pikachu and Raichu give 100 percent in battle!

Raichu is the evolved form of Pikachu but, so far, Ash's Pikachu has chosen not to evolve!

This is all part of what makes Ash's Pikachu special. In some ways, it's no different from other Pikachu. Still, its strong friendship with Ash is what sets it apart and makes it happy.

Team Rocket thinks that Pikachu is special, too. They have tried to steal Ash's Pikachu almost since the moment he got it. That's what Team Rocket does; they steal other Trainers'

Team Rocket causes trouble almost everywhere they go!

Pokémon. However, no matter how many times Team Rocket has tried to grab Ash's Pikachu, the two friends are always reunited.

Strangely, Pikachu and Team Rocket have ended up working together a few times. On one occasion, Pikachu lost its memory and Meowth convinced Pikachu that it had been a member of Team Rocket since it was a baby! Pikachu thought that the members of Team Rocket were its friends. When Ash came to rescue Pikachu, it didn't recognize him at first. Luckily, their deep friendship helped Pikachu regain its memory!

Meowth and Pikachu have met on several occasions!

Bonsly and Mime Jr.

Another tim
Pikachu and
Meowth got
lost together.
If that wasn't
strange enough,
the two of them wandered onto the
set of a TV show starring Bonsly and
Mime Jr. When Jessie found Pikachu
and Meowth, she cooked up a devious
money-making scheme.

Jessie and Meowth planned to
substitute Brock's Bonsly and Team
Rocket's Mime Jr. for the stars of the
show, who were missing at the time.

However, this was all a plan to kidnap Pikachu.

When Ash and his friends came to find Pikachu, they got caught up in star fever for a moment. In the end, they eventually brought Pikachu safely out of Team Rocket's clutches!

Pikachu and Meowth face off again!

Bold Pikachu has tried many new things, like surfing, ping pong, and even entering a Pokémon fashion contest with Ash!

Pikachu is one talented little Pokémon. Once, it showed that it could imitate others.

Pikachu imitates another Pokémon—can you guess which one?

During a talent contest, Pikachu imitated the facial expressions of other Pokémon. It was so good at imitations that Pikachu became one of the top finalists in the contest!

Does Wobbuffet look familiar?

Pikachu has learned many things during its adventures with Ash, including the value of a strong friendship.

Through difficult times and tough challenges, through victories and defeats, Ash and his Pikachu have kept their great friendship alive. The strong connection is what makes Ash a great Pokémon Trainer. It also makes Pikachu a Pokémon that any Trainer would be proud to have!

Index